# A GUIDE TO ハワイのポピュラーな木へのガイド
# HAWAII'S POPULAR TREES

When Mother Nature turned her attention to the Hawaiian Islands, she created a unique living laboratory of flora and fauna unlike anything on earth. The ancestors of Hawaii's present plants and wildlife were brought here by wind and water or carried as seeds by birds, in many cases from islands and atolls long since submerged. In the absence of competition from other plants and animals, they evolved into species unique to these islands. It has been said that had Charles Darwin visited Hawaii before the Galapagos Islands, he would only have written about Hawaii!

Unfortunately, with a few notable exceptions, Hawaii's plants are not particularly spectacular and so attract little support for their conservation or cultivation. Consequently, Hawaii's gardens, streets, and parks are filled with exotic tree species from all over the world. Although a few trees, such as the kukui, coconut, and possibly the hala, were introduced from the South Pacific by the early migrating Polynesians, most of Hawaii's popular trees were introduced after the islands' discovery by Captain James Cook in 1778. They can be found wherever man has seen fit to change his environment.

This guide is intended as an introduction to the amazing assortment of trees to be found in Hawaii.

レインボー・シャワー
### RAINBOW SHOWER
*Cassia javanica x fistula*
Tropical Asia

This hybrid, produced in Hawaii many years ago, is one of the most beloved trees in the islands. Although colors vary from almost white to deep pink, the form known as "rainbow shower" has a profusion of magnificent flowers with petals of pink, orange, and red. The Golden Shower (*Cassia fistula* L., Tropical Asia, ゴールデン・シャワーの木) has orange-yellow flowers followed by huge, pendulous pods up to 2 feet long. These trees are at their best from spring to fall, when they are a common sight along the streets of Honolulu.

オヒア・レフア
## OHI‘A-LEHUA
*Metrosideros collina* (Forst.)
Gray ssp. *polymorpha*
Hawaii

This colorful and abundant native tree is the first woody plant to establish itself on new lava flows, where it remains a stunted bush. But with more soil and moisture, it can reach 80 feet or more in height. Its petal-less flowers are composed of a large mass of brightly colored stamens. Picking these flowers upon entering mountains is said to bring rain because it upsets the goddess Pele. The flowers are also an important source of nectar for Hawaii's rare endemic birds.

3

オオギバショウ
## TRAVELLER'S TREE
*Ravenala madagascariensis* Gmel.
Madagascar

With its enormous leaves that form in the shape of a fan on top of its tall trunk, this plant looks like a huge, flattened banana. In fact, it is a relative. Huge, green, boat-like bracts arise from the leaf axils and enclose the whitish flowers. It is said that fresh water can always be found at the base of the leaves, hence its common name, traveller's tree.

蘭の木
## ORCHID TREE
*Bauhinia Purpurea* (L.)
India and China

The orchid-like flowers of this 20-foot tree and its many related species have given rise to the name "Poor man's orchid." This strong plant will tolerate quite poor, dry soil and is a popular landscape tree in Hawaii. The showy flowers, red-dish purple to maroon, are produced throughout the spring and summer months.

**KUKUI** ククイ
*Aleurites moluccana* (L.) Willd.
Pacific, Tropical Asia

Because it is so abundant and well-known, few Hawaii residents would believe that the kukui is not a native tree. It was first imported by the early Polynesians because of its many uses. Kukui nuts are rich in oil and were used as candles or made into leis. The roots and shell of the fruit yield a black dye. When baked, the kernels are edible, but when raw make a potent laxative.

## KOA コア
*Acacia koa* Gray
Hawaii

The koa tree is highly prized in Hawaii for its beautifully grained wood. This has resulted in the cutting of many of the largest trees for furniture, serving bowls, and decorative pieces. Very large specimens, sometimes up to 50 feet or more, can still be seen in the mountain areas of the island of Hawaii. The koa tree is frequently mentioned in Hawaiian legends and songs.

フクベの木
## CALABASH TREE
*Crescentia cujete* L.
Tropical America

The calabash tree has a short trunk and spreading branches bearing narrow leaves and bell-shaped flowers. The strange round fruit, each between 6 and 12 inches in diameter, are green when young, but turn black when ripe. They are thick shelled and contain many seeds embedded in pulp.

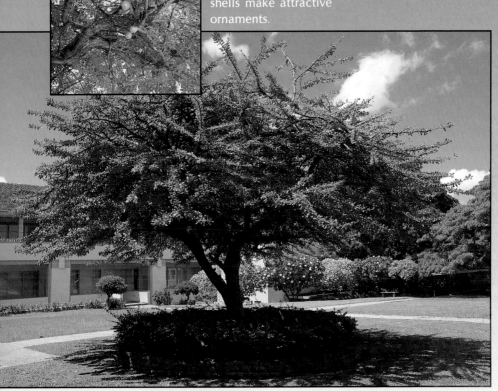

Today, the fruit are sometimes hollowed out and used as rattles. When polished, the shells make attractive ornaments.

スクランブル・エッグの木 ; カラモナ
## SCRAMBLED EGG TREE; KALAMONA
*Cassia surattensis Burm.f.*
*India to E. Polynesia*

This is an attractive and colorful shrub or small tree.

Orange-yellow flowers are borne in continuous profusion at the ends of slender arching branches, reminiscent of scrambled eggs!

The bluish-green leaves are divided into 8-16 pairs of leaflets and flat pods, 2-6″ long, persist on the plant.

The bark is said to be useful in curing diabetes.

ナツメヤシ
**DATE PALM**
*Phoenix dactylifera* L.
North Africa

This famous palm from North Africa has a great many uses. In addition to its well-known edible fruit, the leaves are used for thatching and woven items, and sugar and wine are made from the sap. As the plants are drought tolerant they are invaluable for landscaping in dry areas in Hawaii.

カエンボク
**AFRICAN TULIP**
*Spathodea campanulata* Beauv.
Tropical Africa

From late spring to fall, majestic trees often 70 feet tall can be seen bearing large clusters of erect red flowers on branch tips. This is the stately African tulip, one of the most spectacular of tropical trees. The cone-shaped fruit contain numerous seeds surrounded by papery bracts that are distributed by the wind. Unfortunately, this has enabled the tree to enter some of Hawaii's native forests, where it threatens to become an unwelcome invader.

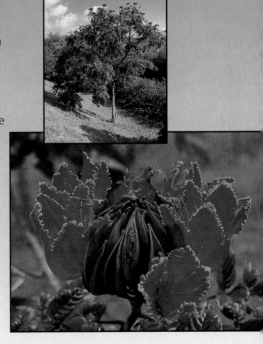

11

ペーパー・バーク
## PAPER BARK
*Melaleuca leucadendron* L.
Southeast Asia to Australia

The bark of this small tree, the source of its common name, is quite spectacular. It peels off in papery layers, creating a most attractive effect. This adaptive tree does well when in boggy locations, and also in drier areas. The wood is used for firewood and fence-posts, and medicines are made from the leaves.

**MANGO** マンゴ
*Mangifera indica* L.
Malaysia

Few have not heard
of the exotic mango,
one of the notable
fruits of the tropics. There
are dozens of varieties in Hawaii, some introduced and
some locally bred.
Opinions vary greatly as
to which is best. The
mango is a large tree,
reaching 70 feet or
more in height. It is an
excellent shade tree.

**GUAVA** グアバ
*Psidium guajava* L.
Tropical America

   Introduced shortly
after Captain Cook's
arrival, the guava quick-
ly gained popularity for
its lemon-shaped, yel-
lowish fruit, which are
produced year-round.
The tree can be easily
identified by its mul-
ticolored trunk, oblong
leaves, and white flow-
ers. The pulp of the
fruit is pink or cream
and can be eaten raw,
but it is more common-
ly used to make the
famous guava juice.

ベンガル・ボダイジュ

# INDIAN BANYAN
*Ficus benghalensis* L.
India

This is the most spectacular of the many banyans in Hawaii because of its massive aerial root system. The roots are produced to support new growth as the tree branches outward. Much of the tree's appeal lies in the maze of passages that the roots of large specimens produce. A banyan at Lahaina, Maui, covers well over half an acre!

## JACARANDA ジャカランダ

*Jacaranda acutifolia* Humb. & Bonpl.
Peru

In late spring and early summer, especially in cooler locations, the jacaranda comes into its own. It bears fern-like leaves and beautiful purple-blue bell-shaped flowers in huge clusters at the ends of branches. These are followed by roundish, wavy, flat-tened fruit.

## PLUMERIA  プルメリア
*plumeria* hybrids

Modern plumerias are hybrids of several tropical American species. They are often called "frangipani" in other parts of the world. The highly scented flowers, produced nearly year round in shades of white, pink, red, and yellow, are prized for leis. The plant possesses an abundance of sticky white juice said to have medicinal properties.

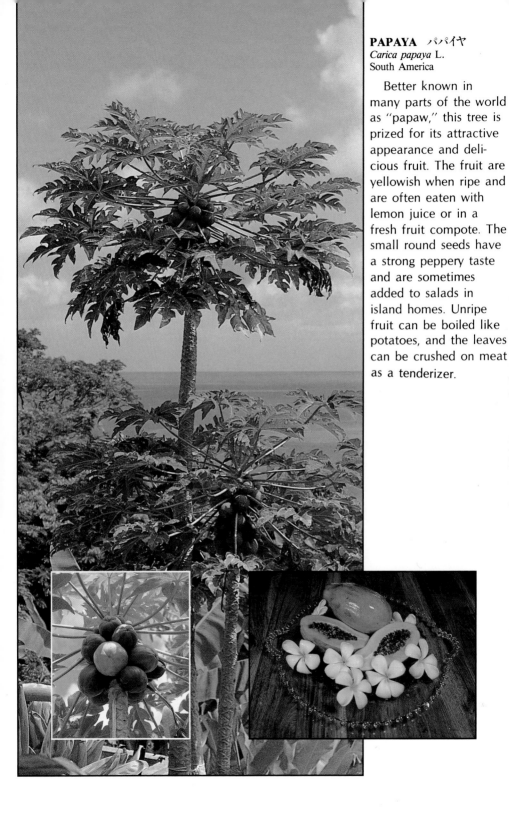

## PAPAYA パパイヤ
*Carica papaya* L.
South America

Better known in many parts of the world as "papaw," this tree is prized for its attractive appearance and delicious fruit. The fruit are yellowish when ripe and are often eaten with lemon juice or in a fresh fruit compote. The small round seeds have a strong peppery taste and are sometimes added to salads in island homes. Unripe fruit can be boiled like potatoes, and the leaves can be crushed on meat as a tenderizer.

## COCONUT ココナッツ
*Cocos nucifera* L.
South Pacific, Tropical Asia

The coconut is one of the most useful plants in the world, producing shade, construction materials, food, oil, bowls, and fiber. It was introduced to Hawaii by the early Polynesians, who had several varieties. Coconut palms can reach a height of 100 feet and, although often growing on sandy beaches with little or no soil, can withstand hurricanes with ease. The mature nuts are enclosed in a fibrous husk, and when ripe they come crashing to the ground. Because of this, mature nuts are rarely seen on trees in public places in Hawaii — they are removed while still young.

**PINK TECOMA**　ピンク・テコマ
*Tabebuia pentaphylla* (L.) Hemsl.
Tropical America

Pink tecoma is a popular island tree. It is distinguished by its profusion of pink flowers, borne in small clusters at branch tips and produced at intervals throughout the year. The trees are especially beautiful when grown as single specimens on lawns, the fallen petals creating a pink carpet beneath the tree.

## COFFEE コーヒー
*Coffea arabica* L.
Tropical Africa

This shrub or small tree with glossy oval leaves bears pure white, strongly scented flowers. A plant in full bloom in late spring is a spectacular sight. After flowering, small, oval red berries or "beans" are produced. They must be harvested by hand as they mature unevenly. *Coffee arabica* is the source of the famous **Kona** coffee from the island of Hawaii. Both flavorful and expensive, it is enjoyed by connoisseurs the world over.

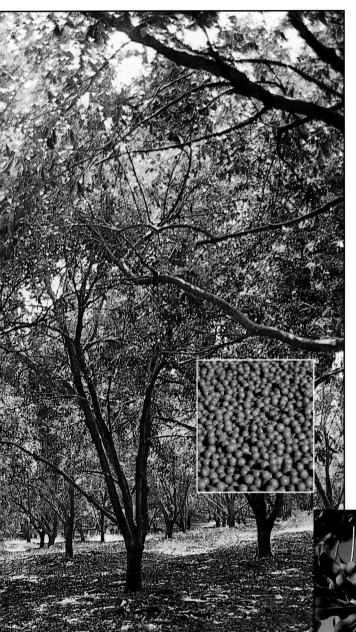

マカデミア・ナッツ

**MACADAMIA NUT**
*Macadamia integrifolia* Maiden
and Betche
Australia

Although widely grown in other parts of the world, the macadamia has become synonymous with Hawaii. The first trees were planted in 1890, but only in the last twenty years have the nuts become an important part of Hawaii's economy. The round, hard-shelled nuts are about 1 inch in diameter. They are harvested from the ground after falling naturally.

## AVOCADO アボカド
*Persea americana* Mill.
Tropical America

The avocado, prized
for its strong-tasting
fruit, was an early in-
troduction to Hawaii.
By careful selection
among the many varie-
ties, one can have fruit-
ing trees almost all year
round. The trees yield a
useful oil and some
parts have medicinal
properties.

ホウオウボク
## ROYAL PONCIANA
*Delonix regia* (Bojer) Raf.
Madagascar

Facing extinction in
its native land, this species was "saved" by
horticulturists, who
planted it in tropical
countries worldwide.
The spreading tree loses
all or most of its fern-
like leaves in early
spring, to be followed
by a blaze of red flow-
ers and new green
leaves. Appropriately, it
is called "flamboyant"
in many parts of the
tropics.

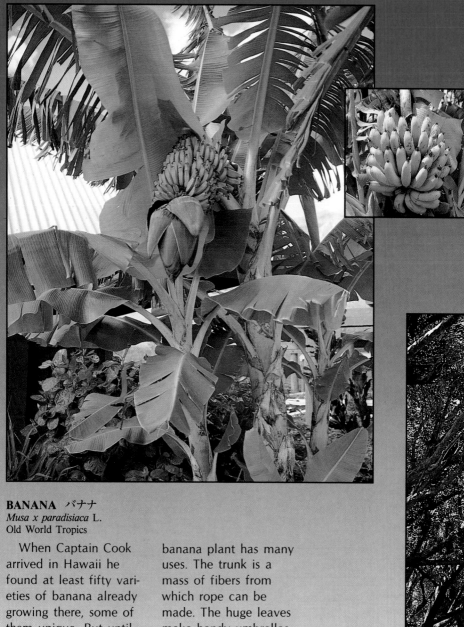

## BANANA バナナ
*Musa x paradisiaca* L.
Old World Tropics

When Captain Cook arrived in Hawaii he found at least fifty varieties of banana already growing there, some of them unique. But until the "kapu" was broken in 1819, women were permitted to eat only two kinds of banana. Like the coconut, the banana plant has many uses. The trunk is a mass of fibers from which rope can be made. The huge leaves make handy umbrellas, plates, or thatch, and have many other uses. After fruiting the trunk dies, but new shoots arise from the base.

## MAHOGANY マホガニー

*Swietenia mahogani (L.) Jacq.*
S. Florida & W. Indies

A handsome tree often more than 60 ft. high with large buttress roots at the base. It is a popular street and landscape plant in many tropical areas.

The shiny leaves are made up of 4-8 pairs of leaflets, each 1-3″ long. Flowers, small and white, are borne in profusion at the ends of wide-spreading branches. The flat winged seeds, from which this tree is most easily grow, are contained in a 2-4″ long woody capsule.

Mahogany wood is prized for many uses including the manufacture of furniture and musical instruments.

## アメリカネムの木
## MONKEYPOD
*Samanea saman* (Jacq.) Merr.
Tropical America

Monkeypod wood is known to most poeple from the beautiful carved bowls and ornaments found everywhere in Hawaii. Less familiar is the tree, with its huge umbrella shape and massive trunk. Its feather-like leaves close up in the evening and in rainy weather, giving it an alternative common name, "rain tree." Another unusual trait is that most trees lose most or all their leaves early in the spring.

## アンブレラ・ツリー
## UMBRELLA TREE
*Brassaia actinophylla* Endl.
Australia

This odd-looking tree has large umbrella-shaped leaves made up of several long leaflets at the ends of branches. When in flower, long, widely spreading floral branches bearing unique small clusters of red flowers have given it the name "octopus tree." The seeds germinate readily and can often be found growing in the forks of large trees or on the ground. For this reason they are unpopular with gardeners, who have to contend with the rapidly growing plants.

**HALA** ハラ
*Pandanus odoratissimus* L.f.
Pacific to East Asia

This strange branching tree can be seen along the shores of all islands. Its long narrow, spine-edged leaves, aerial roots, and large fruits resembling pineapples all combine to make this a most unique and primitive tree. The leaves, "lauhala," are used in making mats, sandals, hats, and baskets throughout the Pacific. They can also be used for thatching.

29

パンの木
**BREADFRUIT**
*Artocarpus altilis* L.
Malaysia

Dozens of varieties of breadfruit are found throughout the Pacific, and the early Polynesians brought one form to Hawaii. The warty-skinned fruit can weigh up to 10 pounds. They are more or less oval and about 10 inches long. The tough outer skin covers a soft pulp flesh that is quite delicious when baked or steamed.

ソーセージの木
**SAUSAGE TREE**
*Kigelia africana* Benth.
Tropical West Africa

The sausage tree is an oddity in Hawaiian gardens. Its strange flowers are reminiscent of raw meat. They are followed by long, broad sausage-shaped fruit, which are inedible although said to be of medicinal use in Africa.

金の木
**GOLD TREE**
*Tabebuia donnell-smithii* Rose
Central America

From early in the year to July or August, tall leafless trees covered with masses of yellow flowers can be seen along streets and highways. This is the famous "gold tree." Only after flowering are the pale-green leaves produced.

# INDEX